How to Write Your Own Wedding Vows and Toasts

DISCARD

A Workbook for Brides
And the Men Who Love Them

written by

TWO HEARTS IN LOVE

Robert Kiefer and Carol Ponder

ISBN 978-1-935271-32-1

First edition, November 2009

Back cover photo: Mario Covic

Every effort has been made to trace copyrights on materials included in this publication. If any copyrighted material has been included without permission and due acknowledgment, proper credit will be inserted in future printings after notice has been received.

Printed in the United States of America on acid free paper.

Robert Kiefer and Carol Ponder
www.vowsandtoasts.com

Published by Westview, Inc.
P.O. Box 210183
Nashville, Tennessee 37221
www.publishedbywestview.com

For Lauren and Bobbie

Love will find a way.

Acknowledgements

This book owes its genesis to three people: first, to Belinda Leslie, who brought Robert to a meeting of the Tennessee Wedding and Event Specialists Association (TWESA, pronounced TWEEZA). At that meeting, Robert met Elaine Parker, the grande dame of Nashville wedding planners. When she first heard Robert's idea about helping people write and rehearse their wedding vows and toasts (as part of his public-speaker/coaching enterprise), she said, "You must write a book." After that, Angie Commons of Premier Bride approached Robert to say, "You must go national with this idea immediately!" Without the inspiration of these three extraordinary wedding professionals, this workbook would not have happened. Here's how to reach them:

Belinda Leslie, proprietor of *Top O'Woodland*, can be found at *www.Topofwoodland.com*. We think that this is the coolest venue in the South for weddings of up to 100 guests.

Elaine Parker owns *Weddings with Elan* and she can be reached at *www.weddingswithelan.com*. Elaine is the premier Tennessee wedding planner and works throughout the country.

Angie Commons is the Nashville marketing director for Jacob Marketing, Inc., which publishes "Premier Bride" in Nashville.
Reach her at *angie@premier-bride.com, www.premierbride.com* or *www.thepinkbook.com* (her blog).

Many other people have encouraged us, answered questions, shared stories, taken time to give thoughtful feedback, offered advice, and generally supported our undertaking. We wish to thank especially Rev. Battle Beasley, Eric Booth, Elizabeth Bush, John and Janie Chaffin, Dr. Bill Compton, Bonnie Arant Ertelt, Elena and Seth Grossman, Amy Dawn Harwell, Dr. Jane High, Gary Hoff, Mary Kathryn Israel, Ben and Ethel Jones, Richard Kiefer, Roxanne Kiefer Mollo, Amanda Luther, Thomas Mollo, Mary Catharine Nelson, Eleanor Israel Ponder, Judy Sebren, Aharon Shamash, and Dr. Barbara Whiteman.

Special thanks go to Em Turner Chitty, who helped us realize that punctuation is a resting place not a destination.

Also, we wish to thank our two seven-and-a-half-pound Maltese (real bruisers) Killer, Descendent of Wolves and Conan the Barbarian, aka Nanners. Woof.

Table of Contents

Introduction

Have you ever been at a wedding reception where someone who's had a little too much to drink hogs the microphone, droning on and on about the wedded couple, telling every single thing he knows about them, suitable or not? Or listened to a younger brother tell a *really* inappropriate story about the groom, followed by the loudest and most embarrassed silence imaginable? (Fortunately, the articulate grace of the father of the bride salvaged the moment.) We have written this book because we don't want the same thing to happen to you!

Which best man's toast would you rather hear at your wedding reception?

Example A: **TRUE STORY (Really!)**

…Not only does Charles drive too fast, he has some other bad habits that Leigh needs to watch out for. When Charley and I were little boys, we used to take baths together and he would, well, let me just say that he used to leave "floaters" in the water, if you know what I mean. Don't want *that* to happen again…

(You can't make this stuff up… We were there – AACKKK!)

Example B: **What might have been.**

…Before Leigh came into his life, Charley mostly cared about his car, his mustache, and his balance sheets. Leigh has taught him to love with his whole heart and to become his best self. Our family would like to thank her for it. Ladies and gentlemen, will you join me in a toast to Leigh and Charles in hopes that they shall bring each other great joy, comfort, and support for all the years to come. Hear, Hear!

We think most of us would agree that Example B is the better choice!

> Love is composed of a single soul inhabiting two bodies.
>
> *-Aristotle*

Got it! But shouldn't you start with your wedding vows?

Yes, absolutely. The wedding vows do come first because without the vows, there's not a wedding, just a great party. You'd never know that, though, by reading most newspaper articles. They describe everything about a wedding **except the centerpiece – the wedding vows.** Make your vows the spiritual and creative center of all your wedding plans – from the color of the flowers to the lace on the ring bearer's pillow. Your wedding day will be based on love and hope and not the length of the sleeves on the bridesmaids' dresses or how big the men's boutonnières are! Our step-by-step process will lead you safely though the challenge of writing your own vows, or personalizing traditional vows.

You plan an <u>un</u>traditional wedding. Is this book suitable for you?

Yes, indeed! Whether you are planning to be married in a church, in a park, by your favorite tree in your backyard, on top of a mountain, on the open sea, or with a Justice of the Peace, this book can help you think through why you want to be married and how to put those feelings into words for your vows. You can take the step-by-step questions in this book, and adapt them to any style of wedding or any venue you choose. Two good friends, psychologists Bill Compton and Barbara Whiteman, were married on the open sea as the captain of the boat blew a whistle to summon dolphins to sing for them. They took their vows from Native American writings. Bill and Barb agree that this book will be helpful to couples, no matter what kind of wedding plans they envision. It is also suitable for use in any religion or faith in which personal, created vows are appropriate and permitted.

> Gravitation can not be held responsible for people falling in love.
>
> -Albert Einstein

Will this workbook help you learn how to *say* your vows?

Yes, it will. Another common frustration we've all experienced is attending a beautiful wedding, where it's clear that the participants have created a meaningful event, but we can't **hear** the bride and groom exchange their vows. How can we be witnesses to their union if we can't hear them? The simple, step-by-step rehearsal techniques found in this workbook can fix this problem.

After you and your fiancé have written unique, heartfelt vows, we will lead you through the rehearsal process – *and* give you ways to calm your nerves on your wedding day.

Can we help your family and friends write and deliver the toasts at your reception and other wedding events?

Of course! We've written a whole chapter devoted to writing appropriate and meaningful toasts and tributes. This workbook will help family or friends give the same care to their toasts that you give to your vows. It will help them add a personal, creative touch to each event associated with your wedding day.

Take note now: What's appropriate for the bachelor and bachelorette parties – where the risqué or funny stories belong – would not be appropriate for the wedding reception or rehearsal dinner. We will help your friends figure out which stories belong at which events.

How do you use this book?

We recommend skimming through the whole workbook, just to get a sense of the whole experience. Then, you and your fiancé simply write your vows using the step-by-step process presented here. Identify other people who will need this book; we recommend that you make it available to anyone who wants to speak at any wedding event. We will guide all of you, from best man through the last groomsman, or maid of honor through the last bridesmaid, through the creative process of crafting the perfect words needed for each occasion.

Keep in mind that we are not disclosing some deep, dark secret: We are simply leading you, step by step, through the same creative process you are already using to make your wedding distinctive and special – *you already know how to do this*. Even more important, if you and your fiancé honestly answer all your questions in this workbook, and put your heart into your vows, *then you will have words to live by, a foundation for the rest of your lives together.*

Do you have to do this all by yourself?

Of course not! You and your fiancé might want to create your vows together, or you might not. Some couples like to save them for a surprise on the wedding day; other couples like to write them together as a way to grow closer. Sometimes one person will decide to write her or his own vows, while the other is content with traditional vows. You decide. If you're writing them separately, or only one of you is writing original vows, then you might invite your best friend or a family member to go through this process with you. We often have ideas in conversation that we'd never have on our own. However you choose to do it, this process can be even more productive and enjoyable – and less scary – if you share it with someone else.

Do we have any other advice before you start writing?

Yes. **We** were advised by the wedding planners we consulted, all of whom have a great deal of experience, to pass along this caution: In the heightened emotional state leading up to your wedding day, sometimes couples and all those involved in creating the wedding can become angry or frustrated out of proportion to the situation – it's part of human nature. Just be aware of this possibility so you can be sure that no past grudges, disagreements, or irritations creep into the process of writing your vows. If you feel that starting to happen, just put your vows down for a bit and come back later – which is another way to learn how to be together for a lifetime.

There are also ways to make your vows a part of your married life: For example, you can frame your original vows to show to your children – what a great example of how to start a marriage! Don't forget to include them in your album of pictures and other memorabilia.

One of the most romantic ideas we've ever heard came from Ben and Ethel Jones of Asheville, North Carolina, who were married on August 1st, 1947 at 8:00 in the evening. Every year, for many years, Ethel put on her wedding dress and they exchanged vows again at 8:00 PM on August 1st. As of this writing, they are looking forward to their 62nd anniversary. Ethel's arthritis prevents her from putting on her wedding dress now, but nothing will prevent them from reciting their vows to each other again this year and every year.

Why did we decide to write this book?

We feel that we have something special to offer to you and your whole wedding party, including your parents, the best man, the maid or matron of honor, honored guests, your friends, and all the rest. We have been married for almost 30 years, and are still deeply in love with each other. We have learned – and continue to learn – how to make the "long haul" work. As for demonstrating creativity – we are performing and teaching artists who have been writing, acting, singing, directing, and teaching for over 30 years, bringing out the creative best in thousands of colleagues and students of all ages (artists or not). In this book, we put the accumulated creative skills

> You don't marry someone you can live with:
> You marry the person whom you cannot live without.
> *-Anonymous*

of our lifetimes at your service. We can help you cultivate and tap into your own originality to craft and deliver your vows, and we can help your guests unlock their sincerest feelings as they write toasts and tributes for the day. Let us help **you be the experts** who create a wedding that inspires all those who attend to renew their own vows through yours.

One more thought: Please enjoy this process and have fun with it! The ability to make each other laugh is a gift that will help you and your fiancé get through life's trials together. Laughter can lift us out of despair, frustration, or anger faster than anything else we've ever found. Writing your vows is another opportunity to learn to laugh together.

Before you start, here's one very important note.

If your wedding is to be in a house of worship, ask the preacher, pastor, minister, priest, rabbi, madhun, or other officiant whether he or she allows original vows, allows you to add to a traditional vow, or whether he or she insists that you use the order of service that is traditional in that place. Even if you can't use your own vows in the wedding ceremony, this book covers every other event in which you and your fiancé might want to exchange promises or stories, and the rest of the wedding party can still make good use of the sections on toasts, tributes, and rehearsal.

Sonnet 116

Let me not to the marriage of true minds
Admit impediments; love is not love
Which alters when it alteration finds,
Or bends with the remover to remove.
O no, it is an ever-fixed mark
That looks on tempests and is never shaken;
It is the star to every wand'ring bark,
Whose worth's unknown, although his highth be taken.
Love's not Time's fool, though rosy lips and cheeks
Within his bending sickle's compass come,
Love alters not with his brief hours and weeks,
But bears it out even to the edge of doom.
    If this be error and upon me proved,
    I never writ, nor no man ever loved.

-William Shakespeare

CHAPTER ONE: THE BRIDE'S VOWS

Yes, we're repeating the VERY IMPORTANT NOTE: If your wedding is to be in a house of worship, ask the officiant whether he or she allows personal, original vows; allows you to personalize traditional vows; or whether he or she insists that you use only the vows that are traditional in that place.

> Give all to love;
>   Obey thy heart;
> Friends, kindred, days
> Estate, good-fame,
> Plans, credit, and
>   the Muse —
> Nothing refuse.
>
> -Ralph Waldo Emerson

OK. Now you begin the process of writing your vows by answering the questions below. You do NOT have to answer every question! The questions are here to guide your own creative process. You don't even have to answer them in order. Feel free to make up your OWN questions. If you're working with your fiancé, a friend, or family member, work with him or her from the beginning, and START EARLY. Do not wait until the last minute to begin the process. Take your time – remember, you only get one chance to say these words to your beloved in front of your community of witnesses.

Also, you will NOT use all of every answer to each of these questions – if you did, your vows would be 30 minutes long. Think of answering these questions as a mining expedition: You want to uncover lots of ideas so you can select the most romantic and meaningful words for your vows. As you answer these questions, look for stories that show off your fiancé's and your best points. Those are the stories that belong in your vows. There will be time for funny anecdotes at the reception, rehearsal dinner, wedding breakfast, showers, bachelorette party, and other wedding events. For now, think about this: What words do you want him to hear when you vow to spend the rest of your life with him? These questions are broken down into three sections:

> ➤ Part One: Why do you want to marry him?
> ➤ Part Two: What do you promise to bring to this marriage?
> ➤ Part Three: Putting it all together.

Let's get started.

Part One: Why do you want to marry him?

Question 1: When and where did you two meet?
(For instance, was it an accident? Were you introduced? Has the place you met become important to you as a couple? What else?)

_____

_____

_____

_____

> In that book which is
> My memory . . .
> On the first page
> That is the chapter when
> I first met you
> Appear the words . . .
> Here begins a new life.
>   _-Dante_

_____

_____

Question 2: What happened the first time you met?
(Did you know he was "the one"? Did you dislike him at first? Did you fall in love at first sight, or were you unimpressed? Did he do something funny or endearing? What else? This might be an amusing or touching story – this might also end up as part of YOUR toast at the reception instead of in your vows.)

_____

_____

_____

_____

_____

_____

Question 3: What first attracted you to him?
(Was it his hair, or eyes, or mouth? Was it his kindness, playfulness, or laugh?
Was it his spirituality or religious convictions?   What else?)

_____

_____

_____

_____

_____

Question 4: What do you love the most about him now?
(Is it his character, his humor, his interests, the way he makes you feel? Is
there something you love about him that he may not <u>know</u> you love about him?
What else?)

_____

_____

A Chinese Poem
I want to be your friend
**   forever and ever**
When the hills are all flat
And the rivers run dry
When the trees blossom
**   in winter**
And the snow falls in summer
When heaven and earth mix
Not till then will I
**   part from you.**
**   *-Anonymous***

_____

_____

_____

_____

_____

_____

Question 5: When and where did he first say, "I love you?"
(Describe where you were, what it was like...)

_____

_____

_____

_____

_____

_____

> There is no remedy for love but to love more.
> -Henry David Thoreau

_____

_____

_____

Question 6: When and where did you first say, "I love you?" (How did you feel when you first said it, and how did he react?)

_____

_____

_____

_____

_____

_____

Question 7: Does he know how to do his own laundry, cook at least three good meals, and actually use all of his electronic devices? Explain!

_____

_____

_____

When you fish for love, bait with your heart, not your brains.
- *Mark Twain*

_____

_____

_____

_____

Question 8: What is the nicest thing he's ever done for you?

_____

_____

_____

_____

_____

_____

_____

_____

Question 9: What is the nicest thing you've ever done for him?

_____

_____

_____

_____

_____

_____

_____

_____

> Love is the master key which opens the gates of happiness.
> - _Oliver Wendell Holmes_

Question 10: What's the funniest or most endearing thing he does?
(This story might, instead, end up at a shower or party...)

_____

_____

_____

_____

_____

_____

_____

Question 11: How do you have fun together? (Going to sports events, museums, movies, NASCAR? What else? What's the best laugh you've ever had together?)

_____

_____

_____

_____

_____

_____

Question 12: Do you have fun separately?
(How do you work that out? Do you follow different leisure pursuits?)

_____

_____

_____

_____

_____

_____

_____

Question 13: What will your life be like after you're married?
(This is really important. How do you plan to smooth out the bumps in life's highway? How will you recognize the good times and face the bad times?)

_____

_____

_____

_____

> Love seems the swiftest, but it is the slowest of all growths. No man or woman really knows what perfect love is until they have been married a quarter of a century.
> -Mark Twain

_____

_____

_____

_____

_____

_____

_____

_____

_____

Bottom line: Why do you want to marry this man?

_____

_____

_____

_____

_____

_____

_____

_____

_____

_____

> I am my beloved's, and his desire is toward me. Come, my beloved, let us go forth into the field; let us lodge in the villages. Let us get up early to the vineyards; let us see if the vine flourish, whether the tender grape appear, and the pomegranates bud forth: there will I give thee my loves.
>
> *-Song of Solomon 7:10-12*

Part Two: What do you promise to bring to this marriage?

Now that you've thought about how wonderful your fiancé is and why you want to marry him, it's time to answer the tough questions about what you bring to this marriage that will make it a real partnership for life. As the saying goes, "Marriage ain't for sissies!"

Question 1: In what ways are you good for him? What will you do for him?

_____

_____

_____

_____

_____

_____

_____

_____

_____

> You can give without loving, but you can never love without giving.
> -Robert Louis Stevenson

_____

_____

_____

_____

_____

_____

Question 2: A marriage is the blending of two lives together. What are the most important things you can do for this marriage? What strengths do you bring to this partnership?

_____

_____

> Love has nothing to do with what you are expecting to get, it's what you are expected to give- which is everything.
> -*Anonymous*

_____

_____

_____

_____

_____

_____

_____

Question 3: Everybody knows that any crisis met with humor becomes more manageable. What role will humor play in your marriage?
(Remember, it takes empathy to create humor – a walk in the other person's shoes, a change in your point of view...)

_____

_____

_____

_____

_____

Part Three: Putting it all together

> **Think of your vows as having a beginning, middle, and end.**

Believe it or not, the hard part is done. Now all you have to do is choose your best ideas and put them in order. In this way, you create a little work of art that puts together the most important, beautiful words that belong in your sacred vows.

Think of your vows as having a beginning, a middle, and an end. In the **beginning**, you state your intention to marry your beloved, along with some reasons why. In the **middle**, you talk about what brought you together, the special things about him, and why you want to spend the rest of your life with him. At the **end**, you make your promises to him.

Now you start *condensing and distilling* your words into the proper length for your vows. It's a matter of selecting and combining the best words.

OVERVIEW OF THE PROCESS

Step 1: Underline the best of what you've written.

Step 2: Copy down what you've underlined (on the next page).

Step 3: Look for great words from poets, authors, or religious texts.

Step 4: Put all this good material into a format with a beginning, a middle, and an end. Create whole sentences using the very best words and phrases that you gather together.

Step 1: Start by going back and finding the most important, meaningful, beautiful, or romantic words or phrases in what you've already written. _Underline them as you go_. (Resist the urge to underline whole sentences.)

Step 2: Now, go back again and copy down what you've underlined. You're gathering all your best ideas into one place. Here.

_____

_____

_____

_____

_____

_____

_____

_____

_____

_____

_____

_____

_____

Step 3: Look for words from great poets and other masters of the language. Use them! Examples are scattered throughout this workbook, with additional suggestions in a chapter at the end for places to look for more. From this point on, read a few every day. Even if you don't use a quotation, something may inspire your own creativity. Use this page to collect phrases or references about where to find them.

_____

_____

_____

_____

_____

_____

_____

_____

_____

_____

_____

_____

_____

Step 4: You've collected a lot of material. These words and phrases are your basic ideas, your building blocks. Now you start putting them together.

Remember, we said that your vows have three sections: a beginning, a middle, and an end. It can be hard to get each section started, so we have included suggestions for how to start the beginning, middle, and ending parts of your vows. You can use them "as is," or combine them, or let these suggestions spark ideas of your own. As long as you are thinking about what you want your fiancé and all the participants in your wedding to hear on your wedding day, what you ultimately write will be *exactly* what it needs to be.

As you compose your vows, refer frequently to the words and phrases you have copied on the previous pages. If you get stuck, go back to the full answers to the questions. Again, it's a great idea to work with someone else – your fiancé if you're working together, a family member or a best friend – whatever works best for you. One wonderful side-effect is that, through this process, you can draw closer to the person who helps you with your vows.

<u>Recipe for a Happy Marriage</u>

A Good Wedding Cake	1 lb butter of youth
4 lbs of love	1 lb of good looks
1 lb of sweet temper	3 lbs of self-forgetfulness
1 lb of pounded wit	1 lb of blindness of faults
1 lb of good humour	1 pint of rippling laughter
1 tablespoon of sweet argument	1 wine glass of commonsense
1 oz of modesty	

-Anonymous

Here are some examples of how to start the three sections of your vows.

Example I
Beginning: I...(*your name*)...want to marry you...(*his name*)... because _____

_____

_____

_____

_____

_____

Middle: I remember..._____

_____

_____

_____

_____

End: I promise..._____

_____

_____

_____

_____

MORE STARTERS: On the next three pages, you will find three more examples of "starters" for the beginning, middle, and end of your toast. Use them, mix them up, or let them inspire your own.

Example II

Beginning: I...(*your name*)...want to marry you...(*his name*)...for so many reasons:

_____

_____

_____

_____

Middle: Not long after we met... _____

_____

_____

_____

End: Through our lives together, I will..._____

_____

_____

_____

_____

Example III

Beginning: You are brilliant! That's why I...(*your name*)...want to marry you...(*his name*)...

_____

_____

_____

_____

_____

Middle: I'll never get over our first meeting..._____

_____

_____. After that, _____

_____

_____

_____

_____

End: The bottom line, my love, is that I will..._____

_____

_____

_____

_____

Example IV

Beginning: Nothing is stronger than love. I love you...(his name)...and so I...(*your name*)...want to marry you today because... _____

_____

_____

_____

_____

Middle: I knew from the first that we were meant to be together. Do you remember..._____

_____

_____

_____

_____

End: I will always be there for you. Never doubt my love...

_____

_____

_____

_____

_____

Example V
Beginning:" How do I love thee? Let me count the ways…"

_____

_____

_____

_____

_____

Middle: Do you remember… _____

_____

_____

_____

_____

End: "I love thee to the depth and breadth and height my soul can reach…" and so I promise…_____

_____

_____

_____

(Quotations from Elizabeth Barrett Browning's "How Do I Love Thee.")

Where are you in the process?

Have you written your first draft of your vows? If you have, it is a good idea to take a day or two away from what you've written, and then to take another look to see if your vows still seem exactly right. (You may look at them several more times to be sure.) You may also want to take a copy of your vows to the officiant who will perform your ceremony. He or she may offer some valuable advice, and there will be no surprises for either of you on your wedding day!

If you haven't finished writing your vows by the time you get to this page – DON'T WORRY! Many people read through the whole workbook and let it settle for a few days before actually beginning to write. Others write a little at a time. Take things at your own pace and revise to your heart's content.

The next chapter is called "The Groom's Vows." Whether you work together or apart on your separate vows, <u>he</u> needs to start now, too, to make certain he's ready on time! He needs to go through the same writing process that you have.

> Love doesn't make
> the world go 'round.
> Love is what makes
> the ride worthwhile.
>
> *-Franklyn P. Jones*

We started from the point of view of the bride in this book because you, the bride, and your family and friends (possibly with the help of a wedding planner) will probably be doing most of the planning and preparation for the wedding and reception; however, we do know that romantic and equal-opportunity men are out there, and we know that nowadays many couples plan their own weddings together. If he starts first, that's great.

(Does he also cook?)

In any case, turn the page for…

Notes:

_____

_____

_____

_____

_____

_____

_____

_____

_____

_____

_____

_____

_____

_____

CHAPTER TWO: THE GROOM'S VOWS

All right, gentlemen, now it's your turn. These questions will not cover whether your fiancée can throw a perfect spiral pass, or if she knows who won last year's World Series. Your questions are very much like hers, but here's the really good part: If you answer them honestly, then you're set. A few years from now when your wife says that you never talk about how you really feel, you can pull out this workbook and say, "But honey, I already told you why I love you and how much. See? It's all written down in this wonderful workbook we did before we were married." Be advised – this will only work a few times in the course of your marriage, so choose the occasions wisely.

> My most brilliant achievement was my ability to be able to persuade my wife to marry me.
>
> *- Winston Churchill*

Take your time answering these questions. You only get one chance to pronounce your vows before your bride and the witnesses (all the other participants, your gathered friends, and relatives). You want to get them right. You may wish to do this with your fiancée as an opportunity to grow closer. Perhaps you will ask a trusted friend or family member to help you discover your answers or you may be the kind of guy who likes to do this by himself. Any choice is a good choice as long as your answers are honest and heartfelt.

These questions are presented as a guide. You do not have to answer all of them - you can even come up with questions of your own. Think of answering these questions as a mining expedition: You want to uncover lots of ideas so you can have lots of choices. For now, look for stories that show off your fiancée's best points. There will be time for funny anecdotes at the rehearsal dinner, wedding breakfast, showers, bachelor party, and other wedding events. Think about the words you want her to hear when you vow to spend the rest of your life with her. The questions are broken down into three sections:

> ➢ Part One: Why do you want to marry her?
> ➢ Part Two: What do you promise to bring to this marriage?
> ➢ Part Three: Putting it all together.

Let's get started.

Part One: Why do you want to marry her?

(No, you may not answer, "Because her daddy's rich.")

Question 1: When and where did you two meet?

(Was it an accident? Were you introduced? Has the place you met become more important to you as a couple? What else?)

> The wondrous moment of our meeting...
> I well remember you appear
> Before me like a vision fleeting,
> A beauty's angel pure and clear.
> – *Alexander Pushkin*

_____

_____

_____

_____

_____

_____

_____

_____

Question 2: What happened the first time you met?

(Did you know she was "the one"? Did you dislike her at first? Did you fall in love at first sight or were you unimpressed? Did she say or do something funny or endearing? What else? This might be an amusing or touching story – and it might also end up as part of YOUR toast at the reception.)

_____

_____

_____

_____

_____

Question 3: What first attracted you to her?
(Was it her hair, or eyes, or body? Was it her kindness, playfulness, or laugh?
Was it her spirituality or religious convictions? What else?)

_____

_____

_____

_____

> At last I know what love
> is really like.   *-Virgil*

_____

_____

_____

Question 4: What do you love most about her now?
(Is it her character, her humor, her interests, the way she makes you feel?
What else? Is there something you love about her that she may not know you
love about her?)

_____

_____

_____

_____

_____

_____

Question 5: When and where did she first say, "I love you?"
(Describe where you were, what it was like...)

_____

_____

> Love means nothing in tennis, but it's everything in life.
> -Anonymous

_____

_____

_____

_____

_____

_____

_____

Question 6: How did you feel when you first said, "I love you?" How did she react?

_____

_____

_____

> Come live with me and be my love,
> And we will all the pleasures prove,
> -Christopher Marlowe

_____

_____

_____

Question 7: Does she know when to change the oil in her car, how to use a screwdriver, and other mechanical mysteries?

_____

_____

Question 8: What is the funniest thing she does?
(This story might end up at a shower or party...)

_____

_____

_____

_____

_____

_____

Question 9: What is the nicest thing she has ever done for you?

_____

_____

_____

_____

_____

_____

> The little unremembered acts of kindness and love are the best parts of a person's life.
> *-William Wordsworth*

Question 10: What is the nicest thing you have ever done for her?

_____

_____

_____

_____

_____

_____

Question 11: How do you have fun together? (Going to sports events, museums, movies, or NASCAR? What else? What's the best laugh you ever had together?)

_____

_____

_____

_____

_____

_____

It's easy to halve the potato where there's love. _-Irish proverb_

Question 12: How about having fun and pursuing your own interests separately? (How will you work that out?)

_____

_____

_____

_____

_____

_____

_____

_____

_____

_____

_____

Here, take my heart--'twill be safe in thy keeping,
While I go wandering o'er land and o'er sea;
Smiling or sorrowing, waking or sleeping,
What need I care, so my heart is with thee?
                                    -Thomas Moore

Question 13: What will your life be like after you are married?
(This is really important. How do you plan to smooth out the bumps in life's highway? How will you recognize the good times and face the bad?)

_____

_____

Love is space and time measured by the heart.
- *Marcel Proust*

_____

_____

_____

_____

_____

_____

_____

_____

_____

The four most important words in any marriage..."I'll do the dishes."

Bottom line, why do you want to marry this woman?

_____

_____

_____

_____

_____

_____

_____

She walks in beauty, like the night
Of cloudless climes and starry skies;
And all that's best of dark and bright
Meet in her aspect and her eyes.

-Lord Byron

_____

_____

_____

My beloved spake, and said unto me, Rise up, my love, my fair one, and come away. For, lo, the winter is past, the rain is over and gone; and The flowers appear on the earth; the time of the singing of birds is come, and the voice of the dove is heard in our land; The fig tree putteth forth her green figs, and the vines with the tender grape give a good smell. Arise, my love, my fair one, and come away.

-Song of Solomon 2:10-13

Part Two: What do you promise to bring to this marriage?

In some ways, the questions so far have been fairly easy. You are already head over heels in love with her and you know that you want to spend the rest of your life with her. In this next part, you have to look down a longer road and express just what it is you will do to uphold this marriage through all of the good times and all the hard times. It is no accident that most traditional vows cover the whole scope of "For richer, for poorer, in sickness and in health."

Question 1: Imagine that you are already married. How do you see your role in this marriage?

_____

_____

_____

_____

_____

_____

_____

_____

_____

> For one human being to love another; that is perhaps the most difficult of our tasks; the ultimate, the last test and proof; the work for which all other work is but preparation."
> -Rainer Maria Rilke

Question 2: What are the most important things you can do for your wife?

_____

_____

> I have found the paradox that if I love until it hurts, then there is not hurt, but only more love.
> —Mother Teresa

_____

_____

_____

_____

_____

Question 3: A marriage is the blending of two lives together. What are the most important things you can do for this marriage? What strengths do you bring to this partnership?

_____

_____

_____

_____

_____

_____

_____

Question 4: Everybody knows that any crisis met with humor becomes more manageable. What role will humor play in your marriage?
(Remember, it takes empathy to create humor – a walk in the other person's shoes, a change in your point of view.)

_____

_____

_____

_____

_____

> The great question...which I have not been able to answer...is, "What...does any woman want?"
> -Sigmund Freud

_____

_____

_____

_____

> Drink to me only with thine eyes
> And I will pledge with mine;
> Or leave a kiss but in the cup,
> And I'll not look for wine.
> The thirst that from the soul doth rise
> Doth ask a drink divine:
> But might I of Jove's nectar sip,
> I would not change for thine.
> -Ben Jonson

Part Three: Putting it all together

Believe it or not, the hard part is done. Now all you have to do is choose your best ideas and put them in order. In this way, you create a little work of art that puts together the most important, beautiful words that belong in your sacred vows.

> Think of your vows as having a beginning, middle, and end.

Think of your vows as having a beginning, a middle, and an end. In the **beginning**, you state your intention to marry your beloved, along with some reasons why. In the **middle,** you talk about what brought you together, the special things about her, and why you want to spend the rest of your life with her. At the **end**, you make your promises to her and to your marriage.

Now you start *condensing and distilling* your words into the proper length for your vows. It's a matter of selecting and combining the best words.

OVERVIEW OF THE PROCESS

Step 1: Underline the best of what you've written.

Step 2: Copy down what you've underlined (on the next page).

Step 3: Look for great words from poets, authors, or religious texts.

Step 4: Put all this good material into a format with a beginning, a middle, and an end. Create whole sentences using the very best words and phrases that you gather together.

Step 1: Start by going back and finding the most important, meaningful, beautiful, or romantic words or phrases in what you've already written. <u>Underline them as you go</u>. (Resist the urge to underline whole sentences.)

Step 2: Now, go back again and copy down what you've underlined. You're gathering all your best ideas here.

_____

_____

_____

_____

_____

_____

_____

_____

_____

_____

_____

_____

_____

Step 3: Look for words from great poets and other masters of the language and use them! Examples are found throughout this workbook, with more suggestions in a chapter at the end. From this point on, read a few every day. Even if you don't use a quotation, something may inspire you to become a word-smith yourself! Use this page to collect phrases or references about where to find them.

_____

_____

_____

_____

_____

_____

_____

_____

_____

_____

_____

_____

Step 4: OK, you've got a lot of material. These words and phrases are your basic ideas, your building blocks. Now you start putting them together.

Remember, we said to think of your vows as having a beginning, a middle, and an end? On the next pages, there are some simple but effective ways to start each section. Look over all of them before you start.

Refer frequently to the words and phrases you have copied above. If you get stuck, go back to the full answers to the questions. Again, it's a good idea to work with someone else – your fiancée if you don't mind that she will know what you're going to say, or a family member or a best friend if that suits you better. One great side-effect is that, through this process, you can draw closer to the person who works with you.

And in Life's noisiest hour,
There whispers still the ceaseless Love of Thee,
The heart's Self-solace and soliloquy.
You mould my Hopes, you fashion me within;
And to the leading Love-throb in the Heart
Thro' all my Being, thro' my pulse's beat;
You lie in all my many Thoughts, like Light,
Like the fair light of Dawn, or summer Eve
On rippling Stream, or cloud-reflecting Lake.
And looking to the Heaven, that bends above you,
How oft I bless the Lot that made me love you.

-Samuel Taylor Coleridge

Here are some examples of beginnings, middles, and ends for your vows.

Example I
Beginning: I...(*your name*)...want to marry you...(*her name*)...because...

_____

_____

_____

_____

_____

Middle: I remember..._____

_____

_____

_____

_____

End: I promise..._____

_____

_____

_____

_____

Example II

Beginning: I...(*your name*)...want to marry you...(*her name*)..for so many reasons:

_____

_____

_____

_____

_____

Middle: Not long after we met... _____

_____

_____

_____

_____

End: Through our lives together, I will..._____

_____

_____

_____

_____

Example III

Beginning: You are brilliant! That's why I...(your name)...want to marry you...(her name)...because everything about you is... _____

_____

_____

_____

_____

Middle: I'll never get over our first meeting... _____

_____

_____

After that, _____

_____

_____

_____

End: The bottom line, my love, is that I will... _____

_____

_____

_____

_____

Example IV

Beginning: Nothing is stronger than love. I love you...(her name)...and so I...(your name)...want to marry you today because... _____

_____

_____

_____

_____

_____

Middle: I knew from the first that we were meant to be together. Do you remember... _____

_____

_____

_____

_____

End: I will always be there for you. Never doubt my love..._____

_____

_____

_____

_____

Example V

Beginning: "How do I love thee? Let me count the ways…"

_____

_____

_____

_____

_____

Middle: Do you remember… _____

_____

_____

_____

End: "I love thee to the depth and breadth and height my soul can reach…" and so I promise…_____

_____

_____

_____

_____

(Quotations from Elizabeth Barrett Browning's "How Do I Love Thee?".)

Where are you in the process?

If you've written your first draft, it's a good idea to take a day or two away from what you've written, and then to read your vows again to see if everything still seems just right. You also might want to take this copy of your vows to the officiant who will perform the ceremony. He or she can offer some valuable advice that could make your vows even more meaningful – and there will be no surprises for either of you on your wedding day!

If you haven't finished writing them by the time you get to this page – DON'T WORRY! Many people choose to read through the workbook to let their ideas mature before they actually begin to write. Take your time and rework your words as much as you wish.

Sonnet 18

Shall I compare thee to a summer's day?
Thou art more lovely and more temperate:
Rough winds do shake the darling buds of May,
And summer's lease hath all too short a date;
Sometime too hot the eye of heaven shines,
And often is his gold complexion dimm'd,
And every fair from fair sometime declines,
By chance or nature's changing course untrimm'd:
But thy eternal summer shall not fade,
Nor lose possession of that fair thou ow'st,
Nor shall Death brag thou wand'rest in his shade,
When in eternal lines to time thou grow'st.
    So long as men can breathe, or eyes can see,
    So long lives this, and this gives life to thee.

-William Shakespeare

CHAPTER THREE: TRADITIONAL VOWS WITH YOUR OWN PERSONAL TOUCHES

For aesthetic or religious reasons, you may want to take a traditional vow and make it more personal. All the work that you did answering the "vows" questions can be put to good use here, especially the phrases you pulled out from your original writing in Parts One and Two. Here is an example of a traditional vow:

I…(*your name*)…take you…(*his name*)…to be my wedded husband, to have and to hold from this day forward, for better or for worse, for richer or for poorer, in sickness and in health, to love and to cherish 'till death us do part.

Now, look at two examples of how to personalize these traditional vows. (The new words that we've added are underlined)

I, Leigh, take you, Charles, to be my wedded husband, to have and to hold from this day forward, for better or for worse, for richer or for poorer, in sickness and in health, to love and to cherish, to lift you up when you are down, to support you in all your life's work, and to be the best person I possibly can be for us, 'till death us do part. I promise to laugh with you, to cry with you, to share in your joys and your pains, and to love you until the end of time .

OR

I, Charles, take you, Leigh, to be my wedded wife. The first time I saw you, when you walked across the campus with hair swinging long and the smile on your face that seemed suddenly to be just for me, I knew that you were the one. I knew that I would always want to be with you, to protect you, to stand up for you, and to support you in all your life's work. I take you to have and to hold, from this day forward, for better or for worse, for richer or for poorer, in sickness and in health, to love and to cherish, 'till death us do part.

Here is another example of a traditional vow that you can personalize. The original vow is:

I...(*your name*)...take you...(*her name*)...to be my [optional: "lawfully wedded"] wife, my constant friend, my faithful partner, and my love from this day forward. In the presence of God, our family and friends, I offer you my solemn vow to be your faithful partner in sickness and in health, in good times and in bad, and in joy as well as in sorrow. I promise to love you unconditionally, to support you in your goals, to honor and respect you, to laugh with you and cry with you, and to cherish you for as long as we both shall live.

And here is the same vow with personal touches:

I, Charles, take you, Leigh, to be my wife, my constant friend, <u>my companion through life</u>, my faithful partner, and my love from this day forward. In the presence of God, our family and friends, I offer you my solemn vow to be your faithful partner in sickness and in health, in good times and in bad, and in joy as well as in sorrow. I promise to love you unconditionally, <u>to share all things with you</u>, <u>to encourage you, to walk life's path with you, and to stand with you if you fall</u>, to support you in your goals, <u>to worship with you and raise a family together</u>, to honor and respect you, to laugh with you, cry with you, and to cherish you for as long as we both shall live For, <u>"So long as men can breathe, or eyes can see/So long lives this, and this gives life to thee"</u>.
(The quotation is from Shakespeare's Sonnet 18.)

As we just did above, it is an excellent time when adapting vows to include something from one of your favorite poets or authors. Is there a quotation that captures your philosophy of love and life? Or perhaps a quote from a religious text? You can even include a whole poem, if all of it speaks to you and is appropriate (and short!).

Here is a traditional vow for a civil ceremony, if that's your choice:

(Name), I take you to be my lawfully wedded (husband/wife). Before these witnesses I vow to love you and care for you as long as we both shall live. I take you as you are with all of your faults and your strengths as I offer myself to you as I am with all of my faults and strengths. I will help you when you need help, and I will turn to you when I need help. I choose you as the person with whom I will spend my life.

The following is the same vow after it has been personalized (we started with a quotation from Dante):

"In that book which is my memory . . .on the first page that is the chapter when I first met you appear the words…Here begins a new life." Leigh, my beloved, I take you to be my lawfully wedded wife. Before these witnesses I vow to love you and care for you as long as we both shall live. I take you as you are with all of your faults and your strengths as I offer myself to you as I am with all of my faults and strengths. I will be worthy of the love you have given me and I honor the love that I give to you. I will help you when you need help, and I will turn to you when I need help. I choose you as the person with whom I will spend my life. This is my vow.

Here is a page and a half, if you'd like to work on adapting traditional vows by inserting your own words and choices.

_____

_____

_____

_____

_____

_____

_____

CHAPTER FOUR: NEVER UNDERESTIMATE THE VALUE OF REHEARSAL!

A tourist visiting New York City for the first time asks a street musician, "How do you get to Carnegie Hall?" The musician answers, "Practice, practice, practice."

Many of you may already have been part of something that required rehearsal – perhaps a Christmas pageant, singing in your church choir, or chorus at school. Maybe you have worked with your local community theater, or worked in the performing arts. In every case, rehearsal was what made it possible to get it right. If you are a professional performer, then you remember this saying, "If we can't hear you, it didn't happen." When you recite your vows, you want to nail it, because you only get one chance. So now it really is time to rehearse what you've written.

> Never forget to bring your sense of humor and your capacity for patience.
> *-Skip Gray*
> *"Acting Out of Your Back Pocket"*

After the content of the vows, the most important thing is that they *be heard clearly*. Not everyone is endowed with a big voice, but anyone can make the most of what they have. Remember, the guests at your wedding are not only there to help you celebrate; they are there as witnesses to your nuptials. If they can't hear you, then they cannot be witnesses to your union.

So how do you rehearse? Let's start with Step 1.

Step 1: Start by simply saying your vows aloud while looking into a mirror. You get immediate feedback on whether your facial expression matches your intention. When you say your wedding vows, you are also saying them to yourself, making promises to yourself, as well as to your fiancé. And, besides, you can practice the dirty look you're going to give your little sister when the Preacher asks if anyone knows any reason, "...why these two should not be joined in Holy Matrimony" and she coughs to get everyone's attention.

Step 2: When rehearsing in front of a mirror, it also helps to think of your reflection as your fiancé's face. A wedding is about joining two into one. Speak from your heart to the person in the mirror. That reflection is the person you love and who loves you. Let them know that you want to spend the rest of your life with them. Don't worry about looking silly. You are alone with the mirror, and it *probably* is not one of those talking mirrors from the fairy tales.

Step 3: Volume! You don't have to shout out your vows, but you do have to speak them loudly enough for all to hear. Volume in speaking does not come from straining your throat. It comes from supporting your voice with your breath – and a deep breath also helps to calm your nerves. The proper way to breathe is from your abdomen. Taking a full breath that expands your abdomen will fill your lungs and give you enough air to support your voice.

A simple exercise is to lie on the floor and put a large book on your abdomen. As you breathe in, the book should go up. As you breathe out, the book should go down. Strengthen the muscles that support your breathing by seeing how far up and down you can make the book move (a form of "crunches" that is also good for your back – you'll do a lot of standing on your wedding day). If it doesn't move, then you are breathing from the top half of your lungs and are not providing enough support to speak loudly. Brides, if you have a wedding dress that requires a corset that trusses you up like a Thanksgiving turkey, then maybe you need a microphone! (Robert likes corsets.)

Step 4: Another way to rehearse is with a friend who can give you feedback. Keeping in mind the notion of breathing properly, use this rehearsal to imbue your vows with the importance they deserve. You're not asking your friend to criticize the words you've written, but to help you say them well. You don't want to say your vows in a monotone, so find the important words and give them emphasis by modulating the volume, speed, or pitch of your voice. (Spend some time listening to people around you every day, and notice how *they* emphasize words as they speak.) It's very helpful to underline or highlight these important words as you rehearse. Also, you may find that you wish to make some changes in the words after you hear them out loud. This is fine. It is part of what rehearsal is for.

Step 5: After you have rehearsed in the privacy of your bedroom, or with a trusted friend, find the biggest room you can to continue rehearsing. The parish or fellowship hall at your church, a classroom at school, or your basement are possibilities, or, if this is an outdoor wedding, practice outside (this may also have the advantage of entertaining your neighbors). Try to fill the room or the outdoors with your voice – this is another good time to take a friend along. He or she can tell you:

> ➢ Can you be heard?
> ➢ Can the words be understood?
> ➢ Do you sound as if you're shouting? (You shouldn't.)
> ➢ Are you breathing deeply enough to support your voice?
> ➢ Are you emphasizing the important words?
> ➢ Is there emotion in your voice, face, and body language?

Step 6: If you and your fiancé(e) have written your vows together, then practicing them together may be helpful. It could be an exercise in pure love, but don't let that keep you from giving gentle advice to each other. After all, you will be relying on each other for help and advice for the rest of your lives. This is not a bad time to figure out how that's going to work. (That having been said, <u>listen to this, men</u>: If a man speaks in a forest and there is no woman around to hear him, is he still wrong? The answer is, of course, YES!)

Step 7: It is always wonderful to hear a couple speak their vows without having the lines fed to them by the preacher. If you are going to do this, however, you must practice them <u>a lot</u>. How do you memorize? The simplest way is to start by learning a few words at a time. Below is an example of how to divide your vows for memorizing, with //backslashes// to set off our suggestions for the size of the chunks that you memorize, one at a time.

I, Leigh, want to marry you Charles because // "you don't marry someone you can live with – you marry the person whom you cannot live without"// and I couldn't possibly live another day without you.// I promise to be there for you, no matter what,// through sickness and health, through wealth and scarcity, and anything else the world hands us.// We will stay together, and watch out for each other, and we'll thrive, no matter what.// So, "come live with me and be my love," for I give you the rest of my life.

PLEASE READ THIS BREAKDOWN CAREFULLY

Start by learning "I, Leigh, want to marry you, Charles, because…" Repeat that until you're sure you've got it (it may take 10 or even 20 times – it's remarkable how easy it is to forget someone's name when you're in a stressful situation). Then to that, add the next phrase, "You don't marry someone you can live with – you marry the person whom you cannot live without." Once you can say both phrases together, add a third phrase, and so on, until your vows are memorized.

Don't be surprised if this takes several days to accomplish. Some people can memorize something with one reading, but most people have to really work at it. This is another reason to rehearse early and often. Once you have your vows memorized, say them to your cat, to a tree as you pass by, to the door, to the plumber (well, maybe not the plumber, but you get the idea).

By the way, the quotes in this vow, underlined, are credited to "Anonymous" and "Christopher Marlowe," found on pages 9 and 36, respectively. You do NOT have to say the names of the people whom you are quoting in your vows, but if you have them printed and framed, you might want to acknowledge them (something like "Contributions from Anonymous and Christopher Marlowe").

Do <u>not</u> wait until the week of the wedding to start memorizing please. There are too many distractions at that time. A good time to start is six weeks out from the wedding. Work on them several times a day, every day right up until the day. *When your wedding day arrives, make certain that the maid or matron of honor, the best man, AND the officiant each has a copy of your vows safely at hand in case you can't remember them in the intensity of the moment.* Writing them on an index card, to fit into people's pockets, might be useful. In the end, this wedding is all about your vows. They are the heart and soul of this ceremony that binds you together. Without your vows, it's just a big party.

> May your love be like the misty rain,
> gentle coming in but flooding the river…
> *- Traditional African proverb*

What do you do if you become uncomfortably nervous before or during the ceremony or if you have "stage fright"?

Sometimes folks are just mighty nervous when it comes right down to the day. Sometimes one of you can become so overwhelmed by the solemnity of the event that you suddenly freeze up. In either case, you forget what you were going to say, or perhaps cannot even respond to the officiant if you are being told what to say. Getting married is an emotional event. Many times people get choked up and start to cry. This is normal and you can allow it happen. Everyone will wait for you and be charmed by the expression of how much this moment means to you. One time (and this is our absolute favorite) a man was so overcome by the fact that he was marrying the love of his life that he began running in place and laughing with joy. Of course everything stopped until he was able to continue, but the best part was that the entire congregation experienced his joy with him. He brought down the house.

> Marriage is like a golden ring in a chain, whose beginning is a glance and whose ending is eternity…
> *-Kahlil Gibran*

The deep breathing that you have practiced in order to say your vows loudly and clearly also works here. If you find yourself becoming uncomfortably nervous, stop what you are doing and take three deep breaths (even if you're at the altar). As you exhale, imagine that all of your nervousness is flowing out of you with the air. We know, it's a simple strategy, but it works. Every time. Remember to exhale fully, or you might become light-headed, but deep breathing is the natural, reliable key to overcoming stage fright. Practice it ANY time you begin to feel nervous as your wedding day approaches, and it will become second nature. If you can convince those around you to breathe deeply as well, it may make the whole process go more smoothly.

And remember this. While you are at the altar, you are in charge. If you freeze or become otherwise unable to continue for a moment, don't worry about it. Just stop for a moment and breathe. You are the star of the show. It's not a wedding until you say your vows, so take your time, get yourself back together, and then move on. If something like this happens, it will provide you with stories to tell your children and grandchildren in the years to come (and your pesky little brother will probably get some mileage out of it at the reception).

Notes:

_____

_____

_____

_____

_____

_____

_____

_____

_____

_____

_____

_____

_____

_____

CHAPTER FIVE: TOASTS AND TRIBUTES

This chapter is for anyone who wants to give a formal toast or tribute at any of the events surrounding your wedding. This includes anyone from the best man to your great-aunt Fanny. Share this chapter with them. *Also share the chapter on rehearsal.*

> May the sun bring you new
>   energies by day,
> May the moon softly restore
>   you by night,
> May the rain wash away any
>   worries you may have,
> And the breeze blow new
>   strength into your being,
> And then, all the days of
>   your life,
> May you walk gently through
>   the world,
> and know its beauty and yours.
>
> *Words from a Native
> American Wedding Ceremony*

To those who will be giving toasts: One of the trickiest things about writing and giving toasts is making sure that your toast is appropriate for the occasion. For that reason, we invite you to think ahead to all of the wedding events at which you might want to make a toast or tribute (bachelor or bachelorette parties, rehearsal dinner, showers, wedding breakfast, after-parties, and the big one – the wedding reception).

What is the difference between a toast and a tribute? A toast is a short speech offered to honor someone – for example, the best man's traditional toast or the maid or matron of honor's toast to the wedded couple. A longer toast is sometimes called a wedding "speech." It can include many parts, which we will explore shortly. A tribute is a toast that includes an element of *gratitude* – for example, the groom offers a tribute to his bride and to her family for accepting him and for throwing this great party.

TOASTS

Here's a switch – following are some questions <u>we'll</u> answer for you, before we get to the questions that <u>you'll</u> answer for yourself. As you read these, keep three things in mind:

> ➤ You will think about the occasion of your toast.
> ➤ Your toast will be written down ahead of time.
> ➤ You **will** rehearse your toast.

Part One: Questions We Have Answered for You

Question 1: Why do we give toasts? They serve many purposes:

Honoring the Couple
Among these purposes is to pay respect to the couple, recognizing them as a newly created family, and to wish them well in their new life together.

Creating Shared Community
No matter the age of the wedding couple and their friends, sharing a story or remembering a shared experience through a toast helps bring people together to create a sense of camaraderie. After all, this is the community of people who by their presence at the wedding ceremony promise to support the bride and groom in their new life together. Shared experiences strengthen this community. These stories will be remembered and they become a part of the couple's life together.

Providing Introductions
Another purpose of the toast is to introduce the person about whom you are speaking to those who may not know him or her. For instance, if you're the best man and the bride's family is from across the country and has never met the groom, this is an opportunity to introduce the groom to her family. Make the most of it. Help them see why the bride chose this man, of all others, to have and to hold for the rest of her life. Also, don't forget to introduce yourself!

May there always be work for your hands to do.
May your purse always hold a coin or two.
May the sun always shine warm on your windowpane.
May a rainbow be certain to follow each rain.
May the hand of a friend always be near you.
And may God fill your heart with gladness to cheer you.

- Anonymous

Question 2: Why is it important that <u>you</u> give this toast?

As you've seen in the previous question, a toast can serve many functions; however, we didn't talk about one of the main reasons you might choose to offer a toast – the satisfaction of contributing something personal and beautiful to the wedding day. If you have been asked by a member of the wedding party to give a toast, then they have trusted you to create and present an offering appropriate to the day. If you think you might be moved to offer a toast (when the floor is opened for spur-of-the-moment or less formal toasts) then do some preparation beforehand so that your contribution is also a fitting addition to the festivities.

Question 3: To whom are you giving the toast?

Whether you have been asked by a member of the wedding party to give this toast or have decided you want to offer a toast from the floor (in the time allotted), you are inviting all of the guests to join you in giving it to the bride and groom as a gift.

Question 4: How long should a toast be?

It depends on who you are in relation to the bride and groom. If you are the maid of honor or the best man, then you can spend up to three or even four minutes on a toast if it is a really good one. If you are a guest at the wedding reception and want to wish the couple well, then you should limit your toast to 30 seconds or less. (A lot can be said in 30 seconds if you write it down first.) If you are the father of the bride and are not completely unnerved after adding up how much this whole party has cost you, now is your opportunity to put that behind you for a few minutes and let your daughter know just how much she is loved and how much you want her to succeed in her new life. Then you can head for the bar.

> May your glasses be ever full,
> May the roof over your heads be always strong,
> And may you be in heaven half an hour
> before the devil knows you're dead.
> *- Traditional*

Question 5: How do you choose appropriate material for the occasion?
You have to consider what is suitable for the occasion. For example, the toast that is just a <u>tiny</u> bit off-color and funny might be OK for the wedding reception, but the story about how many girlfriends the groom went through before finding his true love belongs at the bachelor party.

> Three bridesmaids walked into a bar...the fourth one ducked.
> *-Anonymous*

Question 6: Is it OK to use humor?
The most successful toasts we have heard at wedding receptions do include humor, but in such a way that it highlights something special about the couple. ("Three bridesmaids walk into a bar..." is appropriate only for the bachelor party.)

Wedding planner extraordinaire Elaine Parker offers this quick list of things to think about when you are writing your toast.
DO's:
- Introduce yourself.
- Give a little personal history.
- Go for genuine humor (nothing rude or vulgar).
- Include funny anecdotes (NOT "in" jokes, which not everyone will understand).
- Quirky traits are good, if they are not embarrassing.
- Go for tears – the good kind.
- It's about what a great couple the bride and groom are.
- In what ways are they and their love inspiring?
- How is the world a better place now?
- This is a union of families, as well as individuals.
- Will they have awesome kids? (Be sure they *want* kids before using this one).

DON'T's:
- Do not embarrass the people being toasted or the guests.
- Don't insult anyone.
- *Don't* bring up an ex.
- No bad jokes.
- Don't hog the spotlight.
- Remember: It's a toast, not a roast.

> I was married by a judge. I should have asked for a jury.
> *-Groucho Marx*

Question 7: Should you give a toast if you've had too much to drink?

The answer is "**NO!**" You will have written your toast out anyway – PLEASE, give it to someone else to read. You don't want to ruin the reception or rehearsal dinner or any other occasion, especially those at which old and young alike are present. Remember:

Friends don't let friends speak in public drunk!

Part Two: Questions Only You Can Answer

Question 1: If you were asked to give a toast, why? What is your relationship to the wedding couple?

(We don't mean to terrify you [further], but it is a great responsibility to give a toast. Why did they ask **you**?)

_____

_____

_____

_____

_____

_____

> What greater thing is there for two human souls
> than to feel that they are joined together to strengthen
> each other in all labor, to minister to each other in all sorrow,
> to share with each other in all gladness,
> to be one with each other in the silent unspoken memories?
> *-George Eliot*

Question 2: If you are not one of the designated speakers (that is, if you weren't invited to speak by the bride, groom, father, or mother of the bride or groom, or another member of the wedding party), *why* **have** *you decided* **to prepare a toast, and what is your relationship to the wedding couple?**

(This is where the "30-seconds toast" rule comes in. Remember, as we said before, a great deal can be accomplished in 30 seconds if it is written down and well-rehearsed.)

_____

_____

_____

_____

_____

Question 3: What is the occasion of your toast?

If it is the wedding reception, think about Great-Aunt Fanny's sensibilities as you answer the rest of these questions. If it is the bachelorette party, think about Great-Aunt Fanny's pool-boy.

_____

_____

_____

_____

> May the saddest day of your future be no worse than the happiest day of your past.
> *- Traditional*

Question 4: What experiences have you shared as the bride's or groom's friend?
(How many sleepless nights have you spent talking? How many road trips have you taken over the years? How often have you sat for hours, solving the world's problems? What events have defined your relationship?)

_____

_____

_____

_____

_____

_____

_____

Question 5: In what ways are the bride and groom special as a couple?

_____

_____

_____

_____

_____

Question 6: What other questions should you ask yourself?

Above are only some of the questions that can help you approach writing YOUR toast. Can you think of any other questions about your relationship to the couple that might lead you in the right direction? Write down the questions and answers and spend some time looking over everything you've written so far.

_____

_____

_____

_____

_____

_____

_____

_____

_____

_____

_____

_____

As you look at what you've written so far, you may find that the "hook" for your toast becomes clear.

Question 7: What's a "hook"?

A hook is a central idea around which you write. An example might be, "Charles and Leigh create joy wherever they go." Everything, from popular songs (which often have a hook in the chorus) to short stories and novels, has a **central idea**. An observation about the couple or the story of a moment you experienced with them that "says it all" can be a hook. Exploring this central idea or story will determine what you compose.

Write down that central idea or story here.

_____

_____

_____

_____

_____

_____

_____

_____

_____

_____

> May you have warm words on a cold evening,
> A full moon on a dark night,
> And the road downhill all the way to your door.
> *-Traditional*

Part Three: Putting It All Together

Congratulations, you've gotten through the hard part! Now all you have to do is choose the best ideas and put them in order. In this way, you create a little work of art that says exactly what you want to say. What are the most important, beautiful, or humorous things that need to be said by you at the rehearsal dinner or wedding reception? What is better left for the bachelor or bachelorette parties, showers, or after-parties?

Step 1: Now you start *choosing and distilling* your words into the proper shape and length for your toast. Start by first going back and finding the most important, meaningful, beautiful, or hilarious phrases in what you've already written. <u>Underline them as you go</u>.

Step 2: Go back now and write down what you've underlined, here, so all your really good thoughts are in one place.

_____

_____

_____

_____

_____

_____

_____

_____

_____

Now would be a good time to look for words from great poets and other masters of the language, or traditional toasts that have survived the test of time. Use them! Examples are scattered throughout this workbook and, at the end of this book, you will find some places to look for more examples. From this point forward, read a few every day until you're done. Even if you don't use a direct quotation, something may inspire you. Collect phrases or references about where to find them here.

_____

_____

_____

_____

_____

_____

_____

_____

_____

Now you will feel no rain,
for each of you will be shelter for the other.
Now you will feel no cold,
for each of you will be warmth to the other.
Now there will be no loneliness,
for each of you will be companion to the other.
Now you are two persons,
but there are three lives before you: his life, her life and your life together.
Go now to your dwelling place to enter into your days together.
And may all your days be good and long upon the Earth.

-Apache Wedding Prayer

Anything else you'd like to add?

_____

_____

_____

_____

_____

_____

_____

_____

You've collected a lot of material. These words and phrases are your basic ideas, your building blocks, whether you are writing a 30-second toast or a four-minute wedding speech.

As we wrote in the chapters on Vows, think of your toast as having a beginning, middle, and an end. In the beginning, you want to introduce yourself. Remember, there will be people at the wedding who do not know all of the friends of the bride and groom. During this introduction is a great time to include a little history of your relationship to the couple and perhaps a short story to put your words in context. In the middle, focus on the wedding couple and their love for each other. The ending should wrap up all of your stories quickly and lead into a congratulatory raising of the glasses for a toast or a marriage blessing. Take a first crack at a 30-second toast on the next page:

> **Think of your toast as having a beginning, middle, and end.**

Beginning: _____

_____

_____

_____

_____

Middle: _____

_____

_____

_____

_____

_____

_____

End: _____

_____

_____

_____

_____

_____

Now, try a longer toast or wedding speech, if that is appropriate for you (if you have been asked by a member of the wedding party to offer a toast); or, here is some more space in which to edit and refine what you've already written.

_____

_____

_____

_____

_____

_____

_____

_____

_____

_____

_____

_____

_____

_____

_____

_____

_____

_____

_____

_____

_____

_____

_____

_____

_____

_____

On the next page is an example of a wedding speech (basically, a long toast) that was given by Aharon Shamash, who was the best man at the wedding of Robert's cousin Elena to her beloved Seth. It combines toast, tribute, history, humor, and a wish for a life filled with happiness. Aharon had obviously rehearsed it several times and delivered it beautifully – and it came in at exactly four minutes.

Aharon's Toast

Beginning: (introduction) Good afternoon everyone. For those of you who don't know me, I'm Aharon, one of Seth and Elena's close friends from childhood. **(tribute)** For the next several minutes I'm going to tell you a little bit about my friendship with Seth, and about how these two met. First I would like to thank Elena and Seth's families and friends for coming together today and making this wonderful day possible, and I would like to thank everyone for joining Elena and Seth on this special day.

Middle: (relationship to Seth) I met Seth in the 9th grade when I moved to New York. He was in my homeroom class in junior high, and sometimes sat at the same table as I did. We knew each other fairly well, but were not really close friends. I would listen to him ramble on about the Knicks and the Giants and the Rangers; even back then, sports were all that he liked to talk about. **(humorous story)** One day I forgot to do my biology homework and casually asked Seth if he could help me out with a couple of the answers as I rushed to do it in the 15 minutes before biology class. He sneered at me and with his thick coke bottle glasses and braces and joker-like grin said, "I spent a lot of time on this homework, maybe you should have too..." then he said "Good luck with all that." What a guy, huh? Needless to say, it took a couple more years for Seth and me to become really good friends and, for the record, I did get an A minus in biology that year, no thanks to him.

(relationship to couple) I have known Elena for almost as long. She has been a close friend of my sister and my family ever since I can remember. Your beautiful smile and laugh always light up any room, and you are truly one of the sweetest and most genuine people that I know.

(anecdote) At my sister's and my annual Fourth of July party in 2002, Elena and Seth, who had met a couple of times previously, (and had both expressed a casual interest in each other), finally got to hang out one on one, which I must admit was somewhat of a set up by my sister Hela and me. While we all hit it off with drinking games and loud music, Elena and Seth couldn't stop talking to each other, and didn't leave each other's side at all throughout the night. **(hook – central idea)** Amazingly, after the party and after the alcohol wore off, Elena was somehow still interested in Seth, and the rest is history.

(shared experiences) Seth, over the years you have truly become one of my best and closest friends, and I have watched you transform from the selfish and rude 9th grader, who wouldn't assist a fellow classmate with a couple of biology answers, to a caring, genuine friend who really cares about those around him. You also got contacts and a haircut, which were both wonderful improvements. We've been through so much together: Sand Street Beach, hanging out in the "S" section, trips to Rocky Point, Italy, midnight drives to Foxwoods and Atlantic City, "30 Pack" Fridays, arguing about the

Mets and the Yankees, the Jets and the Giants as well as numerous arguments about fantasy baseball and football (at which I do seem to consistently beat you). It has been amazing being your friend over the past 14 years and I would like to thank you for giving me the opportunity to speak here today. There are a lot of wonderful friends of yours here worthy of giving this speech, and I wanted to say thank you for choosing me as your best man; it is truly an honor.

End: Over the past four years you have been through so much together, and I would like to wish you both a lifetime of happiness together from the bottom of my heart. I love you guys and I wish you the best. If everyone would raise their glasses and join me in a toast to the beautiful bride and groom… **(good joke, closing with a laugh)** I'm actually not done yet…Seth, one more thing. If you and Elena ever take a class together, you should probably let her copy your homework.

Notice how Aharon's toast covers most of the questions that we asked you to answer. He is Seth's best friend, and he also effortlessly acknowledges the extent and depth of Seth's many other friendships by thanking him for the honor of being his best man. Aharon starts with a funny story to amuse us, includes many shared experiences, and surprises us with "…one more thing…" after the actual lifting of glasses at the end. Even if you don't want to write a wedding speech, but would rather stick with a 30-second toast, you can mine Aharon's wedding speech for ideas about how to put together your own words and ideas.

Examples of Short Toasts

Sometimes you just want to say a simple, traditional toast, for instance, the famous Irish Blessing, "May you be in Heaven a half hour before the Devil knows you're dead." There are endless websites on the Internet where traditional toasts from different cultures are listed – choose any one that fills your purpose. However, sometimes you may want not only to use a traditional toast, but also to create something personal to go along with it. Here are some examples:

> A book of verse, underneath the bough,
> A jug of wine, a loaf of bread - and thou
> Beside me singing in the wilderness -
> Ah, wilderness were paradise enow!
> -Omar Khayyam

Example I

Charles and Leigh, I've never known a couple so perfectly suited to each other. You were meant to be together, so:
May you have warm words on a cold evening,
A full moon on a dark night,
And the road downhill all the way to your door.

Example II

I've known Charles since we were both in kindergarten and for a long time I was afraid he would never find someone who could appreciate his off-center approach to life, his wacky sense of humor, and his capacity for great kindness. Then Leigh came along, and from the first bad pun I heard her utter, I knew that they were meant for each other. So, here's to Charles and Leigh:

> May the blessings of light be upon you,
> Light without and light within.
> And in all your comings and goings,
> May you ever have a kindly greeting
> From them you meet along the road.

Example III

It is said that there is a soul-mate for everyone – you just have to find yours. The first time Leigh introduced Charles to us, we knew that each had found that true soul-mate. My friends, I am so glad you found each other. May your marriage be long and joyful, and filled with all good things. [As you raise your glass, say,] Here's to Leigh and Charles!

Example IV

Charles and Leigh, here is something that my grandfather used to always say at family gatherings. I think it appropriate to this occasion:

> May your neighbors respect you,
> Trouble neglect you,
> The angels protect you,
> And heaven accept you.
> And may you love each other
> To the end of time. Hear, Hear!

Example V

Something as simple as: "Ladies and Gentlemen, to Leigh and Charles, may they indeed live long and prosper!" will also do quite well if your delivery is heartfelt.

TRIBUTES

As we wrote at the beginning of this chapter, tributes are an expression of gratitude that may or may not be embedded in a toast. This is a wonderful opportunity to thank all of the people who have worked so hard to make this celebration happen: the bridesmaids, the groomsmen, the father and mother of the bride, the father and mother of the groom...you get the idea.

When including a tribute in your toast, understand that it is an expression of thanks on a very personal level. Take the time to recount something special that the recipient of the tribute has done for you or for this occasion. Perhaps asking for ideas from friends will help you find a direction and focus. Ask yourself: What makes this person extraordinary in my life and the lives of those around me?

Sometimes all you have to say is, "Thank you" and you have fulfilled all of the requirements of a tribute. If you need to say more, remember that time is on your side if you are brief and engaging.

Now that you have written your toast and/or tribute, go back to CHAPTER FOUR: NEVER UNDERESTIMATE THE VALUE OF REHEARSAL. Rehearsing your toast is just as important for you as it is for the bride and groom to rehearse their vows. After all, you do want to sound as if you know what you are doing when you get up in front of all those people and start pouring your heart out.

Who should give a toast? When should a toast be given? Who will organize when and where toasts will happen? Ah, we have the magic answer to all of these questions and any others you can imagine. Follow us to CHAPTER SIX!

Notes:

_____

_____

_____

_____

_____

_____

_____

_____

_____

_____

_____

_____

_____

_____

CHAPTER SIX: WORKING WITH A WEDDING PLANNER

What do wedding planners do?
In a big or a small wedding, organization is the key to creativity. Wedding planners help you get organized. They help with all the decisions to be made, from where your wedding will be held to what kind of napkins to order. Even more important, they (or a professional coordinator who works with them) *are present on the day of your wedding to make sure that everything happens as planned.* Your wedding planner will oversee the details so that you are free to focus on the meaning of the day, your families, and the friends and loved ones in attendance.

First and foremost, these women and men have been an intimate part of countless weddings. Value their advice. They have seen what makes a wedding work and what allows one to come apart at the seams. If you want a big wedding, engage a reputable wedding planner. If you want a small, intimate wedding that needs to go off without a hitch (pun intended), engage a reputable wedding planner. If you want to elope, read this chapter anyway – you might change your mind.

If you choose *not* to use a wedding planner, then the rest of this chapter will give you some additional things to think about as you plan your wedding.

How will a wedding planner help you with your vows?
In an ideal world, you would start working on your vows when you start planning your wedding so that your wedding planner can use the ideas, words, and imagery in your vows from the beginning. Your vows can be used to inspire every choice from decorations to dresses as you and your wedding planner design your wedding day together. The wedding planners whom we consulted had great suggestions about how they can help couples who want to write their own vows. (See "Acknowledgements" for their contact information.)

1. At your earliest meeting, tell your wedding planner that you will write your own vows so she can think about it, too. Elaine Parker told us that sometimes only one of a couple may wish to write personal vows. The other may be happy with the traditional vows as written. That's fine. Knowing your intentions gives your wedding planner a good starting point.

2. A good wedding planner will have access to books and publications that will help you to write your vows. (A great wedding planner will suggest that you buy this book.) Wedding planners can also help you find resources on the Internet.

3. While you can expect good advice, you can't expect your wedding planner to write your vows for you. Your vows must belong to you.

4. Another reason to start writing your vows early: Weddings are complicated affairs. If you start creating your vows before you get involved with planning the ceremony, reception, and honeymoon, you have time to reflect on your love. Don't rush. Take the time to get your vows right even as you dive headlong into planning.

5. Your wedding planner can provide another valuable service, which is to remind you that, while you are creating your vows, you must never allow past mistakes, old grievances, criticisms, or any unkind words into the process. Many different emotions may emerge once you have decided to marry, and in the stress and anticipation of the important day, some of those emotions may be unpleasant. These are a natural part of a stressful process, but try to keep that energy out of creating your vows. Work through those troubling thoughts at another time and place. Your wedding planner can offer advice on where and how to do this.

By starting your vows early, you'll be able to share them with your officiant on your first scheduled meeting. When you present them to your officiant, your vows will be in pretty good shape. If the officiant has any changes to suggest or requirements that need to be addressed, you will already have a structure with which to work.

Elaine also emphasized a point that we made at the beginning of this book: DON'T start writing your own vows until you have checked with the officiant who will perform the ceremony, just in case he or she does not allow original vows (in that case, you can use this book just for toasts).

How will your wedding planner help you with toasts?

Keeping in mind that a toast may be welcome at almost any point in the process, from planning your wedding to the actual wedding itself, the majority of toasts will happen at the *rehearsal dinner* and the *wedding reception*. Your wedding planner can be of enormous assistance in making certain that these toasts are well-timed and appropriate.

A reminder: Your wedding planner may be so good and so popular that she is unable to attend your wedding; however, she will provide a trustworthy wedding coordinator to be present at the wedding instead. Your wedding coordinator will see that your wishes are carried out as planned, just as if your wedding planner were there.

Your wedding planner can help you schedule the formal toasts within the festivities and help those giving formal toasts to write and deliver them.

1. At an early meeting, your wedding planner will ask if formal toasts are planned for the rehearsal dinner, the wedding reception, or both. If toasts are planned, then she or he will help you define a schedule and time limits for them.

2. Give your wedding planner the names of all people asked to give a toast. She will make arrangements to meet or to speak with them over the telephone well before the event.

3. If any folks giving a formal toast are concerned about what to say, your wedding planner should first refer them to this book. If they don't want to write their own toasts, then your wedding planner will have a number of short, appropriate examples from which they can select.

4. Your wedding planner will discuss the *timing* of toasts. At the rehearsal dinner, for example, toasts may happen as soon as people are seated and the father of the groom has made his opening remarks, immediately after the dinner, or perhaps following a presentation. For the wedding reception, it's the same. She will help people set the time limits you request and work out a schedule for formal toasts – for example, after the cake-cutting, when everyone is gathered near the cake.

5. Among the things that your wedding planner will take care of are coordinating with the DJ, bandleader, or Master of Ceremonies (MC) to announce and introduce the person giving each toast. She will also – and this is especially helpful – work out an arrangement with the MC, bandleader, or DJ to "pull the plug" on a toast that gets too raucous, too long, or too maudlin. This party is supposed to be fun!

6. You may wish to offer other people in attendance the opportunity to say something spontaneous from the floor. Your wedding planner will help decide the best time for this, help set up a microphone for them to use, or arrange for a cordless microphone. She can also help cut people off if the "open mic" goes on too long.

Great-Aunt Fanny's Toast!

Frequently at weddings, a microphone is passed around so that guests get an opportunity to tell the couple how happy they are for them and to wish them all the best in their new life together. Most of these take 10-20 seconds and some are funny, some are real tear-jerkers. But most of them are along the lines of "Have a great life together." Then they hand the microphone to Great-Aunt Fanny, whom everyone adores. She hasn't been paying any attention to what's been going on because she is the oldest person in the room and she's wondering when the cake is going to be served. Suddenly, someone hands her a microphone. She looks at it, holds it up to her ear as she would a telephone, and says, "Hello?" Enjoy this moment. You, your beloved, and Great-Aunt Fanny will laugh about it together, and the moment will become one of your family's favorite stories.

The thing about passing the microphone is that you are giving up all control over what is said and by whom. If you have no problem with this, then go for it. If, on the other hand, you want to have a little more control over what is happening at your wedding, then your wedding planner should let people know ahead of time that there will be an opportunity for them to speak for up to 30 seconds and that they should prepare their remarks ahead of time.

Another way to shape the "open mic" event is to keep the microphone in one place so that people have to stand up and go to it in front of everybody. This will dramatically cut down on the number of people who speak because so many people are terrified of getting up to speak in public. They will find other ways to wish you well in your marriage.

To find wedding planners in your area who can help you with these challenges and any other questions you have, you can look in the phone book, go online, or ask for advice from a friend who recently got married. Ask for references from other clients from any wedding planner you choose. If you choose to employ one, enjoy the peace of mind that working with a wedding planner provides.

Love has no other desire but to fulfill itself.
But if you love and must needs have desires, let these be your desires:
To melt and be like a running brook that sings its melody to the night.
To know the pain of too much tenderness.
To be wounded by your own understanding of love;
And to bleed willingly and joyfully.
To wake at dawn with a winged heart and give thanks for another
     day of loving;
To rest at the noon hour and meditate love's ecstasy;
To return home at eventide with gratitude;
And then to sleep with a prayer for the beloved in your heart and a
     song of praise on your lips.
                                              -Kahlil Gibran

Notes:

_____

_____

_____

_____

_____

_____

_____

_____

_____

_____

_____

_____

_____

_____

CHAPTER SEVEN: BEAUTIFUL WORDS – POETRY AND PROSE

Throughout this book, we've scattered poems and quotes that you may feel free to use. As promised, here are some websites and books that you may find helpful as you write your own vows, toasts, or tributes.

- **Your public library!** You may go online, if you wish, to search the database for helpful books, but consider going to the library together where a real person will help you narrow your search – and enjoy doing it.
- Do the same thing at your favorite book store.
- *The Norton Anthology of Poetry* and *The Norton Anthology of Modern Poetry* – type these into your favorite search engine (or ask your librarian) for the most recent editions.
- *The Collected Works of William Shakespeare* – any edition. If you have a favorite teacher, she or he might be able to help you narrow your search.
- If you don't have time to read *The Collected Works of William Shakespeare,* simply type "Shakespeare Love Quotes" into a search engine, and many entries will appear.
- Use the Internet. We had great luck finding useful websites by going on-line and typing "love poetry" or "traditional wedding toasts" or "funny wedding toasts" into our favorite search engine. This led us to options too numerous to mention. Narrow the search by thinking about the wedding event for which you are planning. Type in the event, an author, a time period, or anything else that serves your needs.
- Amazon.com. Go to Amazon and enter "Love Poetry Books". Over 4,000 entries will come up, so narrow your search as needed in the same way you narrow your Internet search.

We also advise asking friends and family from multiple generations for their favorite poems or prose of love. You never know what might turn up, and they'll be delighted to help you.

One more thought:
One other option is to hire a *professional speaking coach*. There are many who, for a reasonable amount, will not only help you write your vows, but will rehearse them with you and your fiancé – and any others in the wedding party who want to offer a toast. (Hint: We travel!)

IN CLOSING…

Humor is healing. We use it a lot in this book, because it is one of the power tools in our own marriage. Whether we are both at home in Nashville, Tennessee or one of us is traveling the country working (very often), we talk to each other every day. We also laugh every day, especially when one of us is grumpy or during hard times of any kind.

However, humor is only one face of love. Supporting each other, sustaining each other through adversity, caring for each other through ill health, enjoying each other's company, sharing friends, creating a community of like minds wherever you go – these are some of the wonderful advantages of having a partner for life.

You *will* get angry with each other. Calling a "time out" if an argument gets out of hand is one way to de-escalate the battle. You can make up your own rules for fighting so that there is no irreparable damage; for example, don't let an argument go on for longer than 20 minutes at a time. Make notes about what you really want to say, and don't be sidetracked by an angry retort. Agree to disagree until the next time you discuss the matter under contention. (Sometimes finding something funny in the argument works, but that can backfire. Just ask Robert.) All of these suggestions are simply part of making a loving life together. When we were younger, we scoffed at the idea of never going to bed angry. Now we live by it.

Making love is one seriously soulful way of growing closer to each other, but there will be days, weeks, or sometimes even months when one or the other of you simply isn't up to it because of personal difficulties, poor health, stress, or the challenges of aging. That's when compassion complements passion, and kindness trumps sex appeal. (As my dear husband said to me the other day, "There are a thousand ways to make love, and preparing a cup of tea is one of them." I thanked him and drank deeply.)

Drink deeply of each other. Remember your vows and all the thought that went into them. Find someone who does calligraphy, have your vows copied on great paper, and frame them. Occasionally play the DVD of wedding events, and hear the lovely things people said *about* and *to* you in toasts and tributes.

Above all, love each other, in ways that only the two of you can create together. That's what matters, from this time forward.

Sincerely,

Carol and Robert

Believe me, if all those endearing young charms,
Which I gaze on so fondly to-day
Were to change by to-morrow, and fleet in my arms,
Like fairy-gifts fading away,
Thou wouldst still be adored, as this moment thou art,
Let thy loveliness fade as it will,
And around the dear ruin each wish of my heart
Would entwine itself verdantly still.
It is not while beauty and youth are thine own,
And thy cheeks unprofaned by a tear,
That the fervor and faith of a soul can be known,
To which time will but make thee more dear;
No, the heart that has truly loved never forgets,
But as truly loves on to the close,
    As the sun-flower turns on her god, when he sets,
    The same look which she turned when he rose.

-Thomas Moore

LaVergne, TN USA
19 December 2010
209391LV00003B/2/P

9 781935 271321

[8]